THE GREAT MONSTER JOKE BOOK

THE GREAT MONSTER JOKE BOOK

By Amanda Li

Illustrated by Dan Green

PUFFIN

For Flexigirl and Pretty Kitty
– aka Izzy and Sophia

PUFFIN BOOKS

Published by the Penguin Group
Penguin Books Ltd, 80 Strand, London WC2R 0RL, England
Penguin Group (USA) Inc., 375 Hudson Street, New York, New York 10014, USA
Penguin Group (Canada), 90 Eglinton Avenue East, Suite 700, Toronto, Ontario, Canada M4P 2Y3
(a division of Pearson Penguin Canada Inc.)
Penguin Ireland, 25 St Stephen's Green, Dublin 2, Ireland (a division of Penguin Books Ltd)
Penguin Group (Australia), 250 Camberwell Road, Camberwell, Victoria 3124, Australia
(a division of Pearson Australia Group Pty Ltd)
Penguin Books India Pvt Ltd, 11 Community Centre, Panchsheel Park, New Delhi – 110 017, India
Penguin Group (NZ), cnr Airborne and Rosedale Roads, Albany, Auckland 1310, New Zealand
(a division of Pearson New Zealand Ltd)
Penguin Books (South Africa) (Pty) Ltd, 24 Sturdee Avenue, Rosebank,
Johannesburg 2196, South Africa

Penguin Books Ltd, Registered Offices: 80 Strand, London WC2R 0RL, England

penguin.com
First published 2006
1

Made and printed in England by Clays Ltd, St Ives plc

British Library Cataloguing in Publication Data
A CIP catalogue record for this book is available from the British Library

ISBN-13: 978–0–141–32099–1
ISBN-10: 0–141–32099–0

CONTENTS

YIKES!

AARGH!

EEK!

What's worse than being surrounded by huge scary monsters? Being surrounded by AWFUL JOKES ABOUT MONSTERS, that's what!

Think you can stomach hundreds of gruesome and ghastly gags? Fine, go ahead. But remember:

THIS BOOK IS ENTERED AT YOUR OWN RISK.

Many readers before you have emerged from this experience TREMBLING and SHAKING. Was it with laughter – or pure terror? Find out for yourself. Now say your goodbyes and get ready to enter our madhouse of monster mirth!

A MENACE OF MONSTERS

Monsters, monsters everywhere,
They come out in the night.
So if you want to stay alive,
You best keep out of sight.

What did the monster
say when he met
the human?
'Pleased to eat you!'

What's huge and
hairy and goes up
and down?
A monster on
a pogo stick.

What do you give a
seasick monster?
Plenty of room.

How do you stop a monster
from smelling?
Cut off his nose.

Where do you find monster snails?
On the end of monsters' fingers.

What is the monsters'
favourite football team?
Scream Park Rangers.

What did one of the monster's
eyes say to the other eye?
**'Between you and me there's
something that smells.'**

What would you do if you
saw a blue monster?
Try and cheer him up.

What would you do
with a green monster?
Put him in the sun until he ripens.

Why did the monster spit
out the clown?
It tasted funny.

How do you know if there's
a monster in your bed?
By the big 'M' on his pyjamas.

What's the best way
to see a monster?
From a distance.

What did the grape say when the
monster stepped on him?
Nothing. It just gave a little whine.

Whine!

Where does a monster
sit on the train?
Anywhere he likes!

What do monsters call
human beings?
Breakfast, lunch and dinner.

What should you do after shaking
hands with a monster?
Count your fingers.

What is a monster's
favourite game?
Squash.

What do monster parents say to
their kids during meals?
'Don't talk with someone in your mouth!'

What kind of nurseries do
monster babies go to?
Child scare centres.

Monster 1: We
had burglars last night.
Monster 2: Oh, really?
Monster 1: Well, it makes a
change from beings on toast.

How do baby monsters
like to travel?
By chew–chew train.

What is the monsters'
favourite TV show?
BeastEnders.

What's the first thing a monster
eats in a restaurant?
The waiter.

Monster kid: Mum, is it OK to bring a friend home for lunch?
Monster mum: Yes, fine. Pop him in the oven when he gets here.

Andy: Do monsters smell?
Mandy: Just a phew.

THE FEAR FACTOR

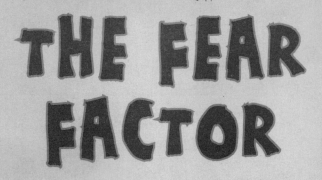

Which scary monster is the scariest of them all? We've spent years making detailed studies of the most fearsome creatures and have come up with a range of revealing ratings – otherwise known as the Fear Factor. So now you can discover which are the beastliest beasts – and, most importantly, how to avoid them…

FEAR METER

THE MUMMY

What makes it scary?

- Ancient, musty and covered in smelly flapping bandages
- Goes 'Uh, uh, uh' and stomps around
- Cannot be reasoned with in any way whatsoever

How to avoid

Don't take up archaeology as your future career.

Top tip

If being pursued by one of these bandaged tomb-dwellers, do not lose your nerve and scream, 'I want my mummy!' The hulking thing will never give up if you do.

FEAR FACTOR: 10/10

VAMPIRE

What makes it scary?
- Big sharp fangs
- Wants to bite your neck and turn you into a vampire just like him
- Lives in a coffin during daylight hours

How to avoid
Hang garlic cloves – loads of them – around your neck. Vampires hate the smell of garlic. Unfortunately, so will all your friends and you'll end up as a Norman No-Mates. Still, it's better than ending up as one of the undead, isn't it?

Top tip
Vampires always wear big black cloaks. If a vampire turns up at your house, it will want to know where the cloakroom is before it gets down to any neck-biting business. Direct it to the nearest broom cupboard and lock it in. If it tries to wheedle its way out, just say, 'No fangs.'

FEAR FACTOR: 9/10

WITCH

What makes her scary?

- Loud cackling laugh and big warty nose
- Flies on a broomstick
- Casts magic spells and makes horrible cauldron concoctions

How to avoid

Keep away from women-only meetings in case the attendees are really witches in disguise. This means you'll never be able to attend one of your mum's Weight Shifters' evenings or become a member of the Women's Institute (aw, what a shame!).

Top tip

Not all witches are evil – some are actually quite nice. It's just a case of knowing which witch is which.

FEAR FACTOR: 9/10

TROLL / GIANT

What makes them scary?
- Very, very big – we mean, like, REALLY HUGE
- Often carries a big club
- Says things like 'Fee, fi, fo, fum' (whatever that means)

How to avoid
You can hear – and feel – their footsteps coming a mile off, so you'll have loads of time to scarper.

Top tip
As giants and trolls are not known for their intelligence, get the better of the great big dimwit by asking it a question. Try something like, 'Hey, giant, what goes "Muf, of, if, eef"?' By the time he's worked out it's a giant going backwards, you'll be home and dry.

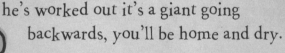

FEAR FACTOR: 8/10

ZOMBIE

What makes it scary?

- Hideous staring eyes
- Lumbering walk
- Rotting flesh
- Uncontrollable urge to strangle any human who happens to get in its way

How to avoid

Simple. Don't hang around graveyards at night.

Top tip

Bits of a zombie (usually the rotting hands) can suddenly drop off, and it may lose its balance and stagger about for a bit. This is your chance to give it a good shove and make your getaway.

FEAR FACTOR: 8/10

CREATURE UNDER THE BED

What makes it scary?

- Lives in the dark shadowy bit under your bed
- Waits until it's night-time and you're alone
- Tries to grab your toes before you jump under the duvet

How to avoid

Wear your slippers right until you've got into bed. Alternatively, buy a futon, which lies flat on the floor, ensuring that there is absolutely NO SPACE for a creature to hide in.

Top tip

No one has yet proved the existence of the Creature Under the Bed. If you managed to capture one, you would therefore become instantly rich and famous. We suggest luring the thing out by dangling your big toe over the edge of your bed (and having a large net at the ready would help). It's toe-tally foolproof!

FEAR FACTOR: 6/10

ABOMINABLE SNOWMAN

What makes it scary?
- It's not a snowman
- But it is extremely 'abominable'

How to avoid
It's only found in the Himalayas, so ask your teacher not to book the Himalayan Holiday Inn as the venue for the next school skiing trip.

Top tip
The creature is known locally as the Yeti, which is a good thing to know if one is trying to eat you. The locals will have no idea what you're talking about if you scream, 'Help! I'm being chased by the Abominable Snowman!' Try shouting, 'Yeti, it get me!' instead.

FEAR FACTOR: 5/10

GIANT SQUID

What makes it scary?

- It's massive
- Loads of tentacles that it can crush entire ships with
- Sprays smelly ink (we're not sure about this, but it sounds really unpleasant so we're keeping it in)

How to avoid

It lives deep in the ocean, so avoid boats, ships and ferry crossings to Calais – even if this does mean missing out on all those super-cheap French hypermarkets.

Top tip

Don't ask for scuba-diving lessons for your birthday, and avoid island holidays.

FEAR FACTOR: 4/10

LOCH NESS MONSTER

What makes it scary?

- Huge, humpy underwater serpent
- Mysterious and elusive
- Thought to be an ancient beast that's as old as the dinosaurs

How to avoid

Don't join the LOONIES (Loch Observation Of Nessie In Evidence-gathering Submarines) or any other of the many crackpot monster-hunting associations that are around.

Top tip

As Nessie only appears once every ten years or so, most people have given up and gone home by now.
We suggest you join them.

FEAR FACTOR: 1/10

BEWARE OF THE DRAGON!

They're green, they're
scaly, they breathe fire!
Black and crispy, you'll expire.

What did the dragon
say to the knight?
'Nice to heat you!'

19

Why do dragons sleep
during the day?
Because they fight knights.

What does a dragon call
knights in armour?
Tinned food.

How do dragons like
their burgers?
Flame-grilled.

Who lives in a land called
Honah Lee and weeps all day?
Puff the Tragic Dragon.

What do you get if you cross
a canine with a dragon?
A hot-dog.

What's a dragon's favourite
breakfast cereal?
Puffed wheat.

What did the mummy dragon
say to the baby dragon?
'You're too young to smoke!'

What do you call a
dragon's ex-girlfriend?
An old flame.

What happens if you get
told off by a dragon?
You get a real grilling.

What do you get if you cross a
dragon with the Big Bad Wolf?
**A creature that huffs and puffs and burns
your house down.**

Why did the dragon breathe
fire on his computer?
He was trying to burn a CD.

What did the dragons hope
for at their barbecue party?
A knight to remember.

What do dragons like
most about school?
Fire drills.

What's green, scaly and
goes up and down?
A dragon on an escalator.

Why do dragons
weigh everything?
They like using their scales.

GIGANTIC
GAGS

Giants and trolls are very large,
Their bums are bigger than a barge.

What should you do if a
giant sits on your car?
Get a new one.

What do you get if a group of
ogres tries on your underwear?
Gi-ants in your pants.

What did the giant use to stop
his trainers from smelling?
Ogre-eaters.

What's huge and scary and
jumps out of lunch boxes?
A bread troll.

How do you know if there's
a giant under your bed?
Your bed is touching the ceiling.

Why did the two giants
go out for a walk?
They fancied an evening troll.

Why did the giant buy
a lottery ticket?
It was a trollover.

What's huge and scary
and hangs around
in bathrooms?
A toilet troll.

What do you call a giant
who's fallen into a pit?
A troll in a hole.

Why did the ogre buy
a new pair of shoes?
He was too big for his boots.

What do you call a giant
with artificial hair?
A big wig.

28

What do you call a giant
who shows off?
A big head.

What do trolls do at night?
They go clubbing.

29

IT'S A MYTH-TeRY!

Legend tells of creatures old,
Whose sight would make your
blood run cold.

What do you get if you cross a
footballer and a mythical beast?
A centaur forward.

Why has a manticore got a lion's
body with a human head?
He's the mane man.

What do you get if you cross
a unicorn with a cobbler?
A shoehorn.

What do you call
a mad unicorn?
A loonicorn.

What do you get if you
cross a basilisk
with a bumblebee?
A buzzylisk.

What do you call a
basilisk with no eyes?
A baslsk.

Have you heard the one about
the half-man, half-horse who
kept showing off?
He had to be the centaur of attention.

Why did Cyclops give up teaching?
He only had one pupil.

What does Cyclops' wife call him?
No eye, dear . . .

What do you get if you
cross a manticore with
a stick of chewing gum?
A minticore.

Where does Medusa get
her snake hair done?
In a Hiss 'n' Hers salon.

Why is Medusa always
at the hair salon?
She's into hair scare.

What's Medusa's hair like?
Coily.

What would you say if you
met a three-headed dog?
'Hello, hello, hello!'

What did one mandrake
say to the other?

Why is a griffin
half-lion, half-eagle?
**So it can roar and soar
at the same time.**

Why do griffins make
excellent spies?
They've got eagle eyes.

What do you call a griffin
with a sore throat?
A gruff-in.

What happened when
Pegasus caught a cold?
He was a little hoarse.

What is Pegasus' favourite
day of the week?
Flyday.

What do you get if you cross a
famous winged horse with
a farmyard animal?
Pigasus.

What did one hideously ugly
winged woman say to the other?
'Don't worry, be harpy.'

Why did the harpy
never get married?
She wanted to stay a myth.

What did one harpy
say to the other?
'Wing you later.'

What game do mythical
beasts play?
Argonauts and crosses.

What did one enchanted
forest say to the other?
'Glade to see you.'

CELEBRITY CREATURES

They're famous all around the nation,
And have a fearsome reputation.

Who's big, green
and very grumpy?
The Incredible Sulk.

Why does the Incredible
Hulk recycle everything?
He's very green.

What's big and green
but keeps turning red?
The Incredible Hulk holding his breath.

What do you get when the Loch
Ness Monster forgets to clean up?
A messy Nessie.

What is the Loch Ness Monster's
favourite nursery rhyme?
'Humpty-Dumpty'.

Has anyone seen the Loch
Ness Monster today?
No, he's got the hump.

What creature can't use
its front-door key?
The Lock Less Monster.

What creature has
always got cold feet?
The Sock Less Monster.

What creature is always
late for school?
The Clock Less Monster.

Has anyone seen the
Abominable Snowman?
Not Yeti ...

Why did the Abominable Snowman
take acting classes?
He wanted to get into snow business.

What do you get if you cross the
Abominable Snowman with a vampire?
Frostbite.

What do you get if you cross the
Abominable Snowman with Tinkerbell?
A hairy, scary fairy.

Could you get rid of the
Abominable Snowman by
throwing eggs at him?
Yes — he'd be eggs-terminated.

What do you call a
monster with a high IQ?
Frank Einstein's monster.

Is Frankenstein's
monster insane?
Well, he has got a screw loose.

Why does Frankenstein's
monster get stomach ache?
He bolts his food down.

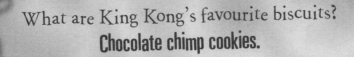

What are King Kong's favourite biscuits?
Chocolate chimp cookies.

How does King Kong make money?
He's in the monkey business.

What hides under the bed
and shakes its thing?
The boogieman.

What hides under the
bed and picks its nose?
The bogeyman.

Why did King
Kong climb to the
top of a skyscraper?
**He was just
monkeying around.**

What does King
Kong wear when
he's cooking?
An ape-ron.

What month
is King Kong's
birthday?
Ape-ril.

What do you get if you cross a cow
with a famous hunchback?
Quasi-moo-do.

Why is King Kong always eating?
He's got a big ape-itite.

Who rings the church bells while
carrying his sandwiches?
The Lunchpack of Notre-Dame.

I Sea, I Sea, I Sea

Heave-ho, me hearties,
and board your fine ship,
But beware of the ocean
and don't take a dip.

What is a sea monster's favourite meal?
Fish and ships.

How do you entertain a baby octopus?
Give it ten tickles.

How much money did the giant
octopus have in the bank?
Six squid.

Why did the sailor disappear?
He'd been squidnapped.

Why do sea monsters avoid eating
ancient ships?
They're as tough as old boats.

Where do sea monsters
keep their money?
In a current account.

How does one sea monster
greet another?
'Good tide-ings!'

Sailor 1: Have you seen any big sharks around here?
Sailor 2: Not a fin.

When do sharks like to eat?
At crunch time.

What do sharks do before bed?
Have a bite-time snack.

Yawn

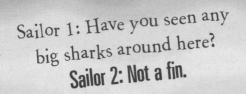

YAK, YAK!

What do you get if you cross a
shark with a parrot?
An animal that talks your head off.

Why should you never
believe a shark?
Because of their fishy tails.

JOKE-OSAURUS

By finding bits of
ancient fossil,
We know that dinos
were colossal.

Why are dinosaurs healthier
than dragons?
Because dinosaurs don't smoke.

What do you get if you cross a
dinosaur with your school uniform?
A Tie-rannosaurus Rex.

What's the scariest
dinosaur of them all?
The Terror-dactyl.

Which dinosaur is the cleverest?
The Thesaurus.

What do you call a healthy dinosaur?
A Well-ociraptor.

Why do people avoid dinosaurs?
Because their eggs stink!

What was the most flexible dinosaur?
Tyrannosaurus Flex.

What do you call a dinosaur
with a bandage on?
Dino-sore.

What do you call a sleepy dinosaur?
A Stegosnorus.

What do you call a dinosaur
that's fallen into a lake?
A Driplodocus.

What do you get if you cross
a dinosaur with a pig?
Jurassic Pork.

What kind of dinosaur gets eaten?
A Dinner-saur.

What do you call a dinosaur that's
been run over by a steamroller?
A Flatosaurus.

TOP TEN WAYS TO GET RID OF A MONSTER

Faced with a ferocious fiend? Attacked by an angry alien? No worries – this user-friendly guide will provide you with everything you need to know in the event of a creature crisis.

1. Divert it. Try tap-dancing or performing a card trick. Can't do either? Just put a pair of pants on your head and run around in circles mumbling. Nobody – not even a terrifying monster – wants to hang out with a weirdo.

2. Offer it a snack. A packet of Monster Munch usually goes down well.

3. Tell it a joke. Not one about monsters, though – they're very sensitive creatures.

4. Do not forget the punch line. This is excellent advice for any joke-telling situation . . . although being eaten alive is not usually a risk in other joke-telling situations.

5. Shout. We suggest, 'Look out, here comes the Phantom Monster-Catcher with His Very Enormous Net for Catching Monsters!' It gets them every time.

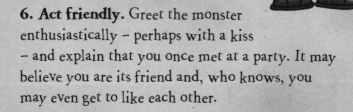

6. Act friendly. Greet the monster enthusiastically – perhaps with a kiss – and explain that you once met at a party. It may believe you are its friend and, who knows, you may even get to like each other.

7. Bore it senseless. Waffle on for hours about your love of train-spotting, pressed flowers, fossil-collecting, etc., etc. The monster may lose interest and wander off.

8. Hypnotize it. You'll need to be a trained hypnotist for this one. Oh well, on to no. 9 then . . .

9. Take it by surprise. Do the unexpected. For example, if the monster attacks, don't fight back but try tickling it instead. At least you'll die laughing!

10. As a last resort . . . If all our advice fails, run like the wind. Get out of there. Jump on your bike and ride. Make like the gingerbread man and run, run as fast as you can . . . (OK, OK, we've got the message.)

SLITHERING SERPENTS

With snakes there's little mystery,
One bite and you are 'hiss-tory'.

What do snakes do after a fight?
Hiss and make up.

What do you get if you cross
a snake with a detective?
A spy-thon.

What do you get if you cross a piece of
garden equipment with a deadly snake?
A mower constrictor.

What sort of knickers do snakes wear?
Ser-pants.

When is a snake like a calculator?
When it's an adder.

What did the serpent
give his girlfriend?
A goodnight hiss.

What did the mummy snake
say to the little snake?
'Viper your nose.'

What do you call a snake on your car?
A windscreen viper.

Why couldn't the snake join the club?
He wasn't a mamba.

What did the snake say to his
long-lost friend?
'Re-mamba me?'

Do snakes ever get embarrassed?
Sometimes they want to coil up and die.

Why was the serpent so popular?
He had a great poisonality.

What is a snake's favourite
football team?
Slitherpool.

IT'S AN ALIEN THING

Little green men come from space,
To scare the pants off the human race.

How does an alien
count to nineteen?
On his fingers.

Alien kids: Mum, Mum,
where's our dinner?
Alien mum: Be quiet, you lot.
I've only got three pairs of hands.

What are aliens'
favourite sweets?
Mars Bars.

Why did the alien
leave the party?
Because there was
no atmosphere.

Where do aliens park
their spaceships?
At parking meteors.

What happened when the astronaut
saw an alien wearing a watch?
He thought it was a lunar-tick.

What do aliens spread on their toast?
Mars-malade or Mars-mite.

Why are aliens so scary?
Because they're extra-terror-estrials.

What's an alien's favourite
day of the week?
Moonday.

What's an alien's favourite game?
Astronauts and crosses.

What do aliens eat
for breakfast?
E.T. bix.

What do you get if you cross
an alien with a wizard?
A flying sorcerer.

What do aliens cook their sausages in?
An Unidentified Frying Object.

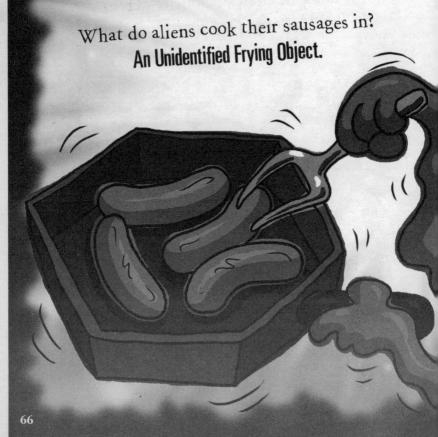

What live on other planets and
are covered in tomato sauce?
Beans from outer space.

Where do aliens catch
their trains?
At the space station.

Why are annoying aliens like bogies?
**They're little green things that get
right up your nose.**

WeReWOLF WANDeRINGS

The moon is full and there's
something scary,
About a beast that is big
and hairy.

What do you get if you cross
a dog with a vampire?
A were-woof.

What are werewolves'
favourite snacks?
Howl-a-Hoops.

Why should you avoid werewolves?
They're barking mad.

Andy: Are there any werewolves
around here?
Mandy: Gnaw idea.

Mandy: What do you get if you
cross a werewolf with a glove?
**Andy: I don't know, but I wouldn't
want to shake hands with it.**

Where do they make werewolf movies?
In Howly-wood.

What do you call a wolf who
lives in a launderette?
A wash-and-wear wolf.

How do werewolves eat?
They wolf their food down.

How do werewolves relax?
They go on howliday.

What do you call a wolf that's been
running around all night?
A weary wolf.

Where do werewolves live?
In werehouses.

What sort of jokes
do werewolves
like best?
Howlers!

MUMMies AND DeADies

Where there's a mummy,
there's a curse,
Which makes things go
from bad to worse.

Why were the ancient
Egyptians confused?
Because their daddies were mummies.

Where do mummies go swimming?
In the Dead Sea.

Why is it safe to tell a mummy a secret?
Because he'll keep it under wraps.

Why was the mummy annoyed?
Someone had been winding him up.

What kind of music do
mummies listen to?
Wrap music.

What do you call a mummy
eating a biscuit?
A crumby mummy.

Mandy: Did the ancient Egyptians
build the pyramids?
Andy: I sphinx so.

What is written on the outside
of a mummy?
'Tomb it may concern.'

Why did the mummy
fail his exams?
He didn't complete his cursework.

What do you call an ancient Egyptian
garage mechanic?
Toot and car man.

Why don't mummies
go on holiday?
They might relax and unwind.

Did you hear the one about the thieves
who broke into a tomb and got covered
in thick brown liquid?
They were gravy robbers.

What did the mummy film director
shout at the end of the day?
'It's a wrap!'

Why do mummies always look
on the bright side?
Because every shroud has a silver lining.

Why are mummies selfish?
Because they're so wrapped up in themselves.

THE BEASTLY BITE CAFE

Hey, monsters – it's munch time at the Beastly Bite Cafe! You won't find a tastier selection of body parts anywhere. So rid yourself of the rumbles and attack these snivelling snacks!

Starter

Marinated being salad

Main courses

Legs – scrambled or terror-fried
Grilled guts with a garnish of gangrene
Spit-roasted rumps – cooked with real spit

Catch of the day

Floundering deep-sea diver, fresh from the sea
(rubber mask and flippers optional)
Warning: bones may be present,
so please take care

Accompaniments

Pickled bunions and corns on the cob
Mashed potatoes (made with real toes)

Desserts

Eyes-cream in various flavours:
shock-olate, boo-berry or vein-illa
Smelly jelly, served with a crunchy
toenail topping

To drink

Limb-onade

BEASTLY KNOCK, KNOCKS

Watch out! There's a monster at your front door . . .

'Knock, knock.'
'Who's there?'
'Goblin.'
'Goblin who?'
'Goblin your food will
give you tummy ache.'

'Knock, knock.'
'Who's there?'
'Harpy.'
'Harpy who?'
'Harpy birthday to you . . .'

'Knock, knock.'
'Who's there?'
'Phoenix.'
'Phoenix who?'
'Phoenix another chip, I'll squirt
ketchup all over him!'

81

'Knock, knock.'
'Who's there?'
'Sphinx.'
'Sphinx who?'
'Sphinx a lot of yourself,
don't you?'

'Knock, knock.'
'Who's there?'
'Witch.'
'Witch who?'
'Witch way do we go now?'

'Knock, knock.'
'Who's there?'
'E.T.'
'E.T. who?'
'E.T. your broccoli
or you won't grow
big and strong.'

'Knock, knock.'
'Who's there?'
'Pharaoh.'
'Pharaoh who?'
'Pharaoh-nuff.'

'Knock, knock.'
'Who's there?'
'Dragon.'
'Dragon who?'
'Dragon your feet wears
holes in your shoes.'

83

'Knock, knock.'
'Who's there?'
'Dino.'
'Dino who?'
'Dino what to do.'

'Knock, knock.'
'Who's there?'
'Vicious.'
'Vicious who?'
'Vicious the way to Amarillo?'

'Knock, knock.'
'Who's there?'
'Adder.'
'Adder who?'
'Adder any more biscuits?'

'Knock, knock.'
'Who's there?'
'Fangs.'
'Fangs who?'
'Fangs ain't what they
used to be.'

TEST YOUR MONSTER IQ

How much do you really know about monsters? It's time to find out with our incredibly detailed and revealing quiz.

1. What's the scariest creature known to humankind?

A A vicious, evil manticore.

B A massive, terrifying basilisk.

C An angry, shouting mum.

2. Why do monsters exist?

A To make money from really bad horror movies.

B To scare the living daylights out of humans.

C Monsters don't really exist, do they?
They do? Yikes!

3. What's the most common kind of nightmare?

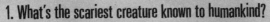

A Being chased by a monster.

B Being eaten by a monster.

C Waking up and realizing you haven't done your homework – oops, I don't actually think that was a dream . . .

4. What would you do if you saw a vampire?

A Chuck some garlic at it.

B Hammer a stake through its heart.

C Ask it round for a bite to eat.

5. Are you scared of monsters?

A Yes.

B No.

C I didn't hear the question –
I was hiding under
my duvet.

Results

Mostly As: Good effort

Your monster know-how is about average. If you'd like to brush up on your knowledge, try a crash course in monsterology, or maybe even a GCSE (Gruesome Creatures Study & Education).

Mostly Bs: Genius

You certainly have what it takes to make it in the monster world . We see a glittering career ahead of you as a top Monster-hunter. Either that or you could write really stupid books about monsters. (Hey! That's my job! – author.)

Mostly Cs: Hopeless case

We really hope you never meet a monster, because if you do you won't last very long. Run and hide!

NIGHT OF THE VAMPIRE

Vampires take a great delight,
In giving folk a juicy bite.

What's a vampire's least favourite meal?
Stake and chips.

What's a vampire's favourite fruit?
Necktarines.

What do vampires write at
the end of a letter?
Best vicious.

Why should you never get
close to a vampire?
They all have bat breath.

Do vampires believe in astrology?
Yes, they always read their horror-scopes.

What does Count Dracula get
from his admirers?
Fang mail.

Did you hear about the two
vampires who had an argument?
They're now the best of fiends.

What sound can you
hear in a graveyard?
Coffin.

Where does Dracula go
when he's in New York?
The Vampire State Building.

How do vampires like their snacks?
Bite size.

Why are a vampire's teeth like stars?
Because they come out at night.

What's red, sticky
and bites people?
A jampire.

What sort of club do
vampires belong to?
A blood group.

What do you get if you cross
a vampire with a duck?
Count Quackula.

Where do vampires go on holiday?
Batlins.

What's it like to be kissed by a vampire?
It's a pain in the neck.

How do vampires sail the seas?
In a blood vessel.

What kind of sausages
do vampires like?
Fangfurters.

Why do vampires
like the circus?
They always go for the juggler.

Mandy: Why do you keep throwing
garlic out of your bedroom window?
Andy: To keep the vampires away.
Mandy: But there aren't
any vampires around here.
Andy: I know. Works brilliantly, doesn't it?

A WHOLE LOAD OF HAGS

Cackle, cackle, see them fly,
Astride their broomsticks
in the sky.

What do you get if you cross
a witch with a fridge?
A cold spell.

What noise do baby witches
make when they are playing
with toy cars?
Broom, broom.

Why do witches use pencil sharpeners?
To keep their hats pointy.

Why do witches use computers?
Because they have spell-checkers.

Why was the witch late?
She'd lost her witch watch.

Why was the witch
shampooing her broom?
She wanted a clean sweep.

What kind of sandals
do witches wear?
Open-toad.

Why won't a witch
wear a flat cap?
There's no point in it.

How can you tell if a witch
is carrying a bomb?
When their brooms tick.

What goes cackle, cackle, bonk?
A witch laughing her head off.

Why did the witch's voice sound hoarse?
She had a frog in her throat.

What do you call a young,
pretty and friendly witch?
A failure.

What would you do if a witch in a pointy
hat sat in front of you at the cinema?
Miss most of the film.

A PILE OF OLD BONES

Hark! I hear a rattling sound,
Coming from the graveyard ground.

Why do skeletons hate the winter?
The cold goes right through them.

What do you call
a skeleton who isn't real?
A bony phoney.

Why are skeletons so calm?
Nothing gets under their skin.

What did one skeleton say to another?
'I've got a bone to pick with you.'

Why didn't the skeleton go to the ball?
He had no body to go with.

Who's the most famous
skeleton in history?
Napoleon Bone-aparte.

How do skeletons travel?
By skelecopter.

What do skeletons do in the evenings?
Watch skelevision.

What do you call a lazy skeleton?
Bone idle.

Why are skeletons cowards?
They have no guts.

Do skeletons ever get scared?
They sometimes get a bit rattled.

What do skeletons write
on their front doors?
There's no place like bone.

Why do skeletons always
order Chinese takeaway?
For the spare ribs.

How do skeletons keep in
touch with each other?
By mobile bone.

GHOSTLY GOINGS-ON

An icy breath, the air is chilly.
Yes, you're being haunted, silly!

What do you call a ghost's parents?
Transparents.

What does a ghost call his parents?
Mum and Dead.

Who was the boy
ghost going out with?
His ghoulfriend.

What do ghosts chew?
Boo-ble gum.

Why are ghosts always relaxed?
They're completely chilled.

What game do ghosts like playing?
Hide and shriek.

Why is 's' a ghost's favourite letter?
Because it turns cream into scream.

What do ghosts do after school?
Watch terror-vision.

What do you call a ghostly cyclist?
Squeals on wheels.

What happened when the boy
ghost saw the girl ghost?
It was love at first fright.

What do you call a ghost
with big ears?
Eerie.

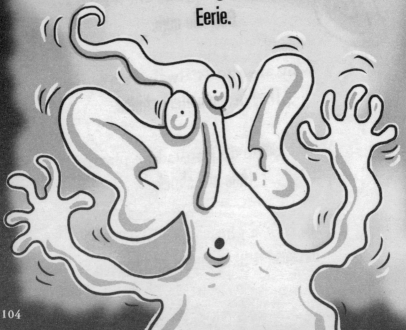

What is a ghost's favourite fairy tale?
'Ghoul-dilocks and the Three Bears'.

What would you do if a ghost
appeared in your bedroom?
Sleep in the living room.

What do ghosts wear to
improve their eyesight?
Spooktacles.

What do you call a ghost
who's good at football?
A ghoulie.

What do ghostly policemen do?
They haunt criminals.

What music do ghosts listen to?
Soul music.

What do ghost drivers wear?
Sheet belts.

What does a boy ghost do
to get a girlfriend?
He wooooooos her!!!

What's a ghost's favourite
day of the week?
Frightday.

1. Watching repeats of *Friends*.

2. Phoning for a vegetarian pizza.

3. Knitting.

4. Going to the library.

5. Visiting a National Trust property.

6. Caravanning.

7. Enjoying a meal in your local restaurant.

8. Making a skoobie keyring.

9. Throwing a pyjama party.

10. Baking muffins.

A MONSTROUS MiX-Up

The beasts would like to welcome you,
To a very mixed-up monster stew.

What do birds do at Hallowe'en?
Trick or tweet.

What do you call
a haunted wigwam?
A creepy teepee.

Why do graveyards
have fences around them?
Because everyone's dying to get in.

Who looks after the graveyard?
A scaretaker.

Mandy: What's the difference
between a coffin and a letterbox?
Andy: I don't know.
Mandy: Well, I won't be asking
you to post my letters then.

Why did the cannibal
eat his father's sister?
He was an aunt-eater.

What did one hideous swamp
monster say to the other?
'Slime to go!'

Why was no one speaking to the
hideous swamp monster?
His name was mud.

What do you call a sick crocodile?
An illigator.

What happened when one giant spider
got married to another giant spider?
They were newly webs.

What's big, green and slimy
with hairy feelers?
I don't know, but there's one crawling
on your shoulder right now!

What did one Venus Fly
Trap say to the other?
'No flies on you.'

What did the fly say when he got
caught in a Venus Fly Trap?
'This is a very sticky situation.'

What did the plant reply?
'Keep your trap shut.'

WHAT KIND OF MONSTER ARE YOU?

If you were a monster, what would you be – vampire, witch, dragon or ghost? Test your monster personality in our really 'fun' quiz.

1. Where would you prefer to live?

A In a damp cave.
B In a spooky castle.
C In a silk-lined coffin.
D In a coven full of cackling hags.

2. What sort of food do you enjoy?

A Anything blackened and burnt to a crisp.
B Frozen food mainly.
C Just a refreshing glass of blood now and then.
D A few warty old toads boiled up in a cauldron.

3. What's your idea of a relaxing weekend?

A Having a super-hot barbecue. Smokin'!
B Just chilling out and finding a new haunt for a couple of days.
C Getting all dressed up and going out on the town for a bite.
D Inviting the girls round for a spellover.

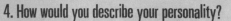

4. How would you describe your personality?

A I'm pretty fiery.

B You can see right through me.

C I like to get my teeth into things.

D Anyone that meets me falls under my spell.

5. What would be your ideal job?

A A chef in a fast-food restaurant – I'd grill the burgers to perfection.

B Working behind a bar – but I'll only serve spirits.

C I'll do anything as long as I can work night shifts.

D A cleaner, so I could use my varied selection of brooms.

Results

Mostly As

Flamin' 'eck! You'd make a red-hot fire-breathing DRAGON.

Mostly Bs

Being a gruesome GHOST is really your thing. Ghoul for it!

Mostly Cs

You were born to be a VAMPIRE. Fangtastic!

Mostly Ds

A spell as a wand-erful WITCH would be just right for you.

ZOMBIE ZONE

Those staring eyes,
that staggering gait,
The zombies are coming
– let's not wait!

What did one zombie say
to the other zombie?
'You must be out of your mind!'

Why do zombies always
look so tired?
They're dead on their feet.

Why did the zombie boy finish
with his zombie girlfriend?
She was too empty-headed.

Who does a zombie
take to a party?
Anyone he can dig up.

What game do little zombies play?
Corpses and robbers.

117

Why do zombies go to school?
To get a good deaducation.

Why is a zombie like an old apple?
They're both rotten to the core.

Why did the zombie jump
out of the wrong hole?
He'd made a grave mistake.

What did the zombie do when
his arm dropped off?
He went to the second-hand shop.

BUY ONE,
GET ONE
FREE!

KNOCK, KNOCK, THERE'S A MONSTER ABOUT!

'Knock, knock.'
'Who's there?'
'Lettuce.'
'Lettuce who?'
'Lettuce in, there's a monster after me!'

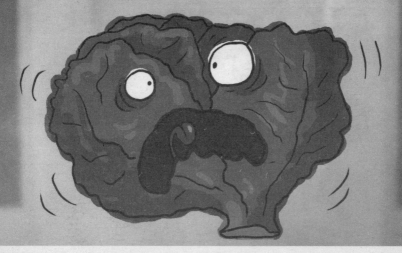

'Knock, knock.'
'Who's there?'
'Shirley.'
'Shirley who?'
'Shirley monsters don't really exist?'

'Knock, knock.'
'Who's there?'
'Ken.'
'Ken who?'
'Ken I come in? I'm scared!'

'Knock, knock.'
'Who's there?'
'Sarah.'
'Sarah who?'
'Sarah way
out of here?'

'Knock, knock.'
'Who's there?'
'Amanda.'
'Amanda who?'
'Amanda the table, shaking!'

'Knock, knock.'
'Who's there?'
'Amy.'
'Amy who?'
'Amy fraid of monsters.'

'Knock, knock.'
'Who's there?'
'Police.'
'Police who?'
'Police open the door and let me in!'

'Knock, knock.'
'Who's there?'
'Luke.'
'Luke who?'
'Luke behind you, there's something horrible!'

And finally . . .

How do you keep a great big horrible monster in suspense? **Tell you tomorrow!**